More Praise for *The Book of Sharks*

In his ambitious collection, *The Book of Sharks*, Rob Carney re-imagines the human world and facets of contemporary society by creating a mythology and origin story that correct the erroneous legend of sharks. In building a new lens through which to view the sea and its most vilified species, Carney opens up a new way to conceive of art, life, storytelling, and the connections among living creatures in the sea, on land, and among the stars. "Some say sharks are the ocean's anger," he repeats in two poems, and later—as the collection evolves—they become "the ocean's blueprint." In this collection, comprised of seven sections, containing seven poems each, Carney weds structure and symbolism to reinforce his creation myth; correction and etymology to reconfigure historical facts; and repetition of images and phrases to place these poems—all without titles, bleeding poignantly into one another as part of an ongoing narrative or interconnected species—in the epic tradition. Here we are offered a sympathetic view of sharks, an alternative way to see constellations and their corresponding myths, and a new foundation from which to begin our lives and our stories. Carney's speaker demands that we reexamine what is actually dangerous versus what's been stereotyped so, and most of all he begs us to see ourselves new, "to bear in mind / we aren't the measure of Creation. Just a part."

—Lisa Fay Coutley

The Book of Sharks

Rob Carney

Black
Lawrence
Press

Black
Lawrence
Press

www.blacklawrence.com

Executive Editor: Diane Goettel
Book and Cover Design: Amy Freels
Cover Art: "Wave VI" by Kazaan Viveiros

Copyright © 2018 Rob Carney
ISBN: 978-1-62557-801-3

Published 2018 by Black Lawrence Press.
Printed in the United States.

Contents

LESSONS

BONES

BONDS

TIDES

ORIGINS

Before mountains rose from the water
and waves ground cliffs into sand,

before rocks rolled down to the shore
and became the first seals,

before that long-ago morning when a cloud
gave birth to seagulls—

white and gray like their mother,
riding the wind—

before storms taught Thunder to waterfalls
and the moon taught Quiet to the snow,

before people and questions
and the names of constellations

there were sharks,
a gliding answer orbiting below ...

their eyes like pieces of the night brought nearer,
their teeth indifferent as the stars,

their purpose the same as the ocean's purpose:
to move, to arrive, to be full.

The oldest carving, though it's yet to be discovered,
is a shark.

Their teeth could be spear points.
Their teeth could be tools.

After bringing back salmon from the river mouth,
after cutting the hide from a seal—

that hide meaning boots through the winter,
a blanket—

somebody stopped to give thanks,
or hoped to turn stone into luck,

or saw lightning carving the sky,
or fashioned an image of the ocean out of love,

out of wanting to please someone.
With a shark's tooth, he shaped the unknowable

into something she could hold, some proof
as sleepless as sharks, abundant as rocks.

And death came fast enough then
that such love probably lasted

at least as long as gratitude lasted,
and longer than good luck.

Some say sharks are the ocean's anger at the sun
for keeping it caught on a line, on a hook

it can't remember biting,
so all its swimming is an endless

circling back.
In their story, the sun is a fisherman,

and the center of the sky is a boat,
and sharks shot forth

from all sudden directions to attack;
they'll take anything close enough.

Most who hold to this version are collectors,
combing the shoreline for teeth

or finding them in tide pools
by turning over crabs.

You'll know them in town by their necklaces
and the jagged bracelets they wear,

by the way they won't enter the ocean.
None of them think their measured streets are nets.

The best explanation I know was offered by a boy.
His father had died, and his mother couldn't hear.

He said, "Sharks are the ocean's way of talking.
Like talking with your hands."

I was just a boy then too.
We were levering boulders

off the cliff point,
watching each splash with satisfaction:

higher than the surf, spraying
halfway back to us.

He said, "Sometimes we just ignore the ocean,
but no one ignores a dorsal fin."

He walked ahead,
and I followed him

to a boulder too big for us to see around.
"If my dad were alive," he said, "he could push this in."

Divers know sharks share the water,
but they dive.

It's as close as they'll ever come to flying,
and the currents below are more likely to grab

and pull down.
The rest of us watch.

We wonder, *How can they do that,*
step out onto that final edge

then leap
and just keep dropping?

Back in town, they seem ordinary
except for the difference in their eyes—

looking under the surface of everything for rocks,
reading each wave of conversation—

some difference . . . horizon . . .
an *apartness* in their eyes.

Like it isn't sharks they watch out for.
Like it's people who normally attack.

Given their name, it should be obvious:
Blue sharks are blue...

even more than you'd think, though.
I've seen one rise to the surface, just appear

alongside the boat, its long nose
out of the water, its eye watching me.

It was June. Summer.
The glacier was calving into icebergs.

The wind had cold spots and warm spots.
The water had a shark—

only four feet long, I'd guess, and skinny as a cat,
but that shark was the bluest thing I'm ever going to see.

There is no body called *Carcharias* we point to in the sky.
They are not our heaven.

We don't pray, "Forgive us our trespasses."
Few of us praise.

But we could if we wanted to.
We could draw from star to star,

teach a son or a daughter, "Those three there together,
that's the fin.

Now follow my arm to that bright one . . .
the five nearby like a sideways V, they're the tail."

It wouldn't take a telescope, wouldn't take a boat,
just lifting a finger.

And each night we'd see that reminder
before we went to sleep.

GATHERING

"What do you do for a living?" is a complicated question
since *for a living* and *for money* aren't the same.

Living means a shoreline is better than a bank vault—
all those deposits of driftwood—

and wealth is measured
by the vivid moments in your life.

Money's just currency,
though it wants to sell you your future.

It has no past, no story explaining the sky,
comparing the stars to a shark bite.

It's plastic littering the sand dunes;
it isn't the grass.

Let's say I'm a gatherer
in the same way clouds are gatherers,

which isn't a ticket to riches
unless you value rain.

Some say sharks are the ocean's anger at us
for being in its future.

They say it knew riptides and hurricanes
wouldn't be enough,

that it would take teeth to teach us, to move us
from selfishness to awe.

Most who hold to this story are quiet,
but they mark the days of past attacks:

a splash of whiskey in their coffee
while they listen to the waves,

listen to the wind chimes they've polished,
then scrub the weather from their porches,

paint their doors.
These chores are their rituals,

performed so you wouldn't even know.
After all, red doors seem common enough,

more like keeping up appearances
than keeping track.

Others focus on a different idea
and spend each April fasting.

That's when coastal waters come alive with food,
nine miles of sardines

and every predator: swordfish
stabbing up from underneath, and birds

harpooning from above,
sea lions, dolphins,

horizons of shark fins. All.
They wait until sundown,

then parade from door to door, trading music
for oysters, a gallon of last year's wine,

and nobody thinks about winter,
nobody thinks about dying.

Only a few of them, the oldest,
hunger for their boats.

In the oldest story we know of, sharks came first:
the perfect idea, perfect shape.

And then the rest of Creation—the sun, the moon,
this planet—to give them a home.

We live on that afterthought,
build boats to crisscross the water,

build churches like islands
surrounded by our cars.

We kill sharks by the millions
and sing along from our hymnals.

In the end, standing at the gates of heaven,
what if we're asked one question: "How are My sharks?"

The best understanding I've heard was offered by a boy.
His father had died of a fever the summer before.

He said, "People think dying
is for every kind of animal but us.

Like it's so unfair we aren't special."
I was just a boy then too.

We'd been trying to climb down the cliff face,
and now we were stuck halfway

with eleven hours 'til light . . .
He looked past his feet

at the water below us,
maybe to add up the distance.

He said, "My dad would have had the guts to jump from here.
He'd have been on the beach already, building us a fire."

Given their name, it should be obvious
what salmon sharks eat.

Still, you never expect it: first a tug
and a sockeye's resistance,

then a *yank*
like the day is having a heart attack.

Just seconds. Only 'til the line
snaps and a gray fin breaks the surface...

The sky isn't the only home of lightning.
The ocean has some too.

I'm a gatherer of what's been gathered:
not like the beach,

more like a kid with a bucket;
not a net,

more a stall at the market, selling fish . . .
or the scale, or the news-wrap.

As purposes go,
it's not a bad purpose to have.

You can be the man buying coho for dinner,
or the woman carrying flowers home for a vase.

I'll be the shelf the vase sits on.
I'll be the tap on the faucet filling it up.

Not the ocean,
just an ear that listens.

Not the shark,
just a gatherer of memories swimming away.

RECONSTRUCTING

FRAGMENTS

The work of a shark is entirely body.
The work of a gatherer is voice;

it's to disappear under the stories
as though they were waves.

A shark follows scent through the water—*Dead Whale*—
and finds a floating month of food.

I come along after the tide's out,
when history's past and memory's an empty lantern.

The electrical field of a shark picks up a thrashing fish
in the distance, and these fragments

I've happened on here and there
are the same.

I have this one dyed onto birch bark:
spearing a shark means seven days of,

and this one carved into cedar:
man with jaws in   window   most afraid.

I have *Catch a shark in your net you have to*
written on a scrap of sheepskin . . .

not stories but maps to the stories.
And so I begin.

Spearing a seal means seven families eat
and seven kids have raincoats,

but spearing a shark means seven days of snow
or heat, depending on the season.

If it's winter, the heat brings avalanches.
If it's spring, the cold takes blossoms

off the trees; so there won't be peaches in August,
no apples to press into cider and distill.

It's a waste,
a breach in need of punishment:

You must drag a driftwood log along the beach,
one side of the harbor to the other,

then saw it—and saw your spear—into pieces
for someone else's fire.

There must have been keepers of knowledge once
in an ancient Order of Ideas

since someone had to chisel the rituals in wood
and carve cold warnings,

since someone needed to know what portions to allot—
what to offer the ground before planting

and give to the ocean as a way of thanking waves
for letting the boats return.

For the dirt, eight pounds from each fisherman's catch
and a weight of clam shells ground into powder.

For the waves, a marlin's liver or thirteen cod,
one for each moon in the year.

As for instructions on feast days:
"Start with a cauldron of seawater."

For warnings?
"Life's eyes are a shark's eyes,

always open
up until the bite."

The man with jaws in his window is the most afraid
he's inessential.

He wants a prop,
a shortcut to identity,

whereas Death knows Its own size already
and doesn't need his bones.

These long-ago scribes would have understood
the edge of the sea is a teacher.

They probably met at the shoreline
to listen to wind

and find what bones
the tide scattered.

The bones of a humpback whale, for instance,
can never be harpoons,

only gaff hooks
for hauling the bulk of a halibut aboard.

They would have considered which uses were worthy
then made sure everyone learned . . .

the way gulls learn that rocks crack crabs wide open,
that hard words are good tools.

Catch a shark in your net, you have to kill it,
understandably. It doesn't know

you want to cut it loose,
that you'd trade a night of mending for its life;

it goes on thrashing, goes on
searching with its teeth.

You have to club it
and club it,

then wait for the air to do its work,
'til it's safe to untangle the body.

It's a terrible hour when it happens.
And each wave slaps like an accusation.

And the hull of your boat is the shape of regret.
You should offer the ocean your knife.

There must have been a Council of Scribes once
making stories like oars to help us row.

We only have fragments,
some passages, but they're enough.

A fin rising out of the water says a shark
is just below the surface,

and warnings, insights, apologies,
occasions chiseled for the record—

these tell me what used to be essential
and should be again.

LESSONS

Before mountains rose from the ocean
so clouds had somewhere to arrive,

before ice carved canyons
and brought the valleys soil,

before seeds taught Color to everything
and Color turned Quiet into birds,

before people and singing
and feathers ornamenting dancers

there were sharks,
indifferent to all of it, celebrating none;

their eyes seeing farther than our firelight,
their teeth needing nothing from our farms,

their lives unimproved by the hides we stretch
into drumbeats,

the ocean a rhythm already,
already their home.

Some say sharks are the ocean's blueprint for tools,
a set of designs for us to imitate.

The great white, for instance, taught us bear traps,
and the thresher's tail taught us scythes

so our corn wouldn't fatten the wilderness,
our cows wouldn't starve.

We'd even have surplus for sour mash
in stills we learned from the whale shark.

And the hammerhead
and the mako's teeth

taught us nails
and how to drive them home.

Most who believe this are carpenters,
and the handles of their saws are stamped with fins.

They could sand a table or a cabinet with sharkskin,
but they won't;

they know they're apprentices,
and what it takes to turn function into beauty,

and respect sharks more than anyone:
the ocean's best design.

In the story once told to warn children, sharks were a curse
called shoreward as a punishment by a witch.

As a girl, she'd been beautiful,
almost as beautiful as vain,

swimming under the moonlight just to be seen,
her clothes flung off along the beach—half taunt,

half invitation. And some looked,
and so they coveted. Others looked

and felt their envy turn to hate,
so loud inside them

they couldn't hear her scream,
thought that sound was their own pitched fury . . .

Though she lived, the girl was disfigured:
an arm

ripped off at the elbow, a leg
torn free.

And the boys just stared, or couldn't look at her,
and the girls made sure she heard them whisper,

'til everyone's bitterness drove the rain away.
The town dried up. The people scattered . . .

Now the witch hobbles up and down the coastline,
watching unseen around corners.

If your image means more to you than anything—
in mirrors, reflected in windows—

then she enters your ear while you're sleeping,
suggests you take a swim.

A blacktip, of course, has black-tipped fins,
but to know that we have to be under the water.

Riding a board across the surface,
we only know the bite.

And hate is no different.
It tells us the ocean's just blue.

Not seaweed green. Not shipwreck.
Not angelfish, anemone, or foam.

And not dark,
the absolute black of space. And no,

not depending on the depth and the weather,
just blue. Hate finds a wave

and starts skimming,
and it feels so buoyant

we can't tell anything is wrong.
We swear along righteously at tiger sharks

though a blacktip bit us,
though it wasn't a tiger at all.

The best explanation I know was offered by a boy.
His father had died, and his mother couldn't hear.

He said, "Anger and the ocean have a lot in common,
and it doesn't have a thing to do with sharks.

It's the size of the water."
I was just a boy then too,

up to my knees in the tide pools.
We were pulling the starfish off mussel beds,

throwing them far,
creating whole solar systems.

He said, "You think your boat will protect you,
that you're crossing it,

and somewhere out there
there's bound to be an island, but..."

He had his dad's knife for prying blue shells from the rocks,
and we'd almost filled our buckets.

Seagulls were full of their screaming song
and balancing on the wind.

"All you've got to drink," he said,
"is what you brought along with you.

Then an empty jug. Then another.
And just the ocean left to fill you up."

Wear charms. Try remedies.
Still, someone dies of a fever. Some boats sink.

I found a shark on the beach:
not starved,

and not bitten,
not corkscrewed open by a boat's propeller,

no hook embedded in its jaw or its gullet,
just dead from ordinary aging.

The sky was unchanged—
a pale light behind the overcast—

no difference in the sound of the ocean.
My friend helped me tow it out

a mile beyond the harbor.
We let the body drift under ... rowed back in.

There is no body called *Carcharias* we look for in the sky.
They are not our heaven.

We name Triton and Pisces,
call a sea of light the Crab Nebula,

but keep sharks away from our telescopes,
out of the stars.

Nobody has to.
We could draw new lines across the night,

teach a son or a daughter, "Those three there together,
that's the fin.

Now follow my arm to that bright one . . .
the eight in a cluster below it, they're the teeth."

It wouldn't take astronomy, wouldn't take a map,
just a little more imagination.

We could add their name to the others
before we went to sleep.

BONES

The cousin of a shark is a manta ray;
and the cousin of a manta ray, a hawk;

and the cousin of a hawk is lightning, the ocean reborn,
returned skyward and alive with storm;

and the cousin of storms is a waterfall;
and the cousin of falling is the wind;

and the cousin of wind is erosion
leaving rock, the bones of the mountains, scattered;

and the cousin of the mountains is a row of teeth,
and another, and another behind;

and those teeth are the cousin of the manta ray,
lightning, the wind . . .

In a story seldom remembered, sharks were ghosts
guarding the afterlife

since their rendered bodies had no skeletons,
just teeth.

The shock of that discovery
must have added new verses to songs

and widened the net of old omens,
but nobody knows. Those details

aren't the details that lasted.
Only this: The dead

step out of their bodies, walk down
to the sea, swim out to the horizon.

For some, the passage is easy—
a day, a night, a warm current there to guide them.

For others, the journey goes on and on—
if they killed a bear, or left a wolf's mate howling—

and the water is cold as a shark's eyes.
And then they see the fins.

Under the first full moon of summer,
they would carry bowls of water,

the light reflected on the surface making more,
a procession of moons moving forward.

In the center of town was a rowboat
being filled one bowl at a time,

and this was the boat of anyone lost at sea,
gone without a burial.

Those in mourning floated candles and petals.
There may have been music on flute or strings,

but we don't know; it's a ritual fallen away,
and all we have left are the wives' tales.

They say their empty bowls filled with quieter sorrow,
and with memories of the dead to carry home.

They say the boat would be gone come sunrise,
just the anchor there,

still as a headstone
by others from the years before.

We have one such anchor on display in the museum,
arrangements of fishhooks,

even spears tipped long ago with sharks' teeth,
and figure, *That's that,*

think the past
fits into our pockets.

We wander about
then buy a bar-code souvenir.

But the past is more like the wind behind us,
and the present more like a ship,

and the only pockets on a ship that matter
are the sails . . .

and they're wrong about the skeletons,
apart from the age of the bones,

bones buried deep but seated upright together,
all of them facing the sea—

so the ancient world believed in guardian spirits
watching over the living,

and a salmon was placed with the deceased
to keep the spirit fed.

Fish bones wrapped in deerskin
were discovered in every grave—

a plausible explanation, but it's wrong.
The living were playing the part of angels,

guiding the dead to the edge of heaven,
seating them upright to find Forever in the waves.

But what about the salmon?
Well, that's counterclockwise too:

The salmon were meant as an offering,
a present for the sharks,

a thank-you for taking our spirits
into their home.

Spearing a shark means seven days of work—
that long to do the rendering—

and all you get is a set of jaws and teeth,
some fragment to hang in a window

or look at over the fireplace
instead of at the fire.

I've heard there are monks somewhere
using human skulls as paperweights.

Not to keep old scrolls from rolling up,
or pages in place while they bind them,

but to bear in mind
we aren't the measure of Creation. Just a part.

The edge of the sea is a teacher—
so many bones:

all the shells and the sand dollars,
all the barnacles encrusted on the pier,

even wood—
it used to stand upright in forests—

even ash left behind in our fire pits
dug to keep warm, to boil water

and empty our crab pots,
even steam rising up like the spirit of rivers,

joining clouds that drift above our graveyards,
and higher still

the moon keeps sailing through its phases,
all of them the color of bone.

BONDS

My friend told stories that weren't real stories at all
the same way the wind's not a song.

We'd be skipping rocks across the inlet
or taking turns with his hatchet,

and he'd tell me, "Orion isn't who you think.
Everyone's looking at him backwards. He's facing left,

and he's a fisherman casting.
My dad taught me all about the stars."

I could see my breath in the January air,
hear the scrape of a shovel clearing snow.

And later that night, I could picture it:
not a hunter's sword but a fishing pole,

not a shield but a stringer of light,
casting the way that my friend saw him casting—

across the distance,
reeling in.

Another time, it was a clump of fur,
barbed wire,

tracks across the orchard.
He said, "Somewhere out there

are drag marks the size of a fawn.
No wonder last night was full of barking.

I wonder if a city kid knows
why apples taste so good."

It was August, hot,
the ditches full from all the irrigating,

and he taught me sometimes all you do is point
since the moment's already a circle.

I followed his finger to a slow procession:
hawks above a tractor.

We watched them, smiling,
as they made their way to the field.

Or it might be three quick words,
their plainness urgent enough,

like the time we'd taken an outboard
just to steal.

It was dark, hours before sunrise,
and we weren't far into the harbor,

and it might have only been driftwood.
We'll never know.

There was a *thump*,
hard,

tipping us, a second
I thought we'd capsize,

and I'd brought along a flashlight,
but he said, "Keep it off."

Just the thought of seeing a fin in the water
and knowing we'd entered that story . . .

we turned around,
stared straight ahead 'til we were home.

Wear charms. Try remedies.
Still, someone goes swimming one morning

and doesn't come back—
maybe drowned, maybe shark attack—

and someone else dies of a virus
swimming in his blood.

I found a crow in my house,
probably down through the chimney.

It traded distrust
for a row of almonds on the floor

and watched cockeyed
while I opened the window . . .

I'd almost forgotten that.
A lot can happen in a year.

Then leaning on the pier one afternoon,
a crow came and landed by my hand.

The cousin of a crow is a raven;
and the cousin of a raven is a myth;

and the cousin of a myth is Story, changing form,
no wave the same shape as another;

and the cousin of a wave is a stingray;
and the cousin of a stingray is a shark,

its eyes as black
as the eyes and feathers of a crow.

His house was always quiet
since his mother couldn't hear,

but the fire she kept going all winter
made it warm, and light

reflected off her photographs:
a sea lion yawning on a buoy;

a whitetip,
rare this close to shore;

a fisherman grabbing at a seagull
flying off, a massive crab in its beak.

At night, through the window,
you could see them glowing.

In the day, they were only black and white.
He said, "My mom already sees the world in color.

The dunes, the town, the marina,
now they're new."

I'm not sure he knew it,
and if he did, he didn't say,

but my friend told stories like his dad
had taught us to fish: "Cast out,

then let your line
do all the talking."

We were working the cove near Bosun's Point.
The trees seemed greener than before.

He told us, "They'll bite, or they won't;
we're together either way."

TIDES

Saturday / 2:07 PST 10.5 ft. / 7:48 PST 3.6 ft.

The work of a shark is entirely body.
The sky's nearest body is the moon.

And the work of the moon is the tides—
pull in, let go.

When they're in, the restaurants are busier.
When they're out, it's time to dig clams,

and tourists here, inlanders, ask about the smell,
frowning at the tide flats.

Sea lions bark. Their noise
carries around the harbor.

Salt wind weathers our houses, scrubs
the names off every mailbox.

An airport shuttle
pulls up to the marina:

three men looking for a charter.
They want to catch sharks.

Sunday / 2:56 PST 9.8 ft. / 8:31 PST 4.3 ft.

When stars are gathered in a pattern,
the word we use is "constellation."

When coral gathers, and anemones,
and fish and eels, we say "reef."

But sharks seen together are "a frenzy"
or one about to start.

Never "meetings," never "congregations,"
never "shopping," not even "a school,"

though they kill less people than lightning
or bath tubs

or cars . . .
just bloodlust and mindlessness.

And a gathering of cars is called "traffic."
And a gathering of drivers is us,

rolling along between billboards,
phones to our ears.

Tuesday / 4:46 PST 8.9 ft. / 10:13 PST 5.6 ft.

Most of us call the Big Dipper by its name.
My friend used to call it The Net

since it had to be there to land salmon
in the life after this—

a dip net of stars
just waiting.

And hopefully sharks in the darkness,
and comets wilder than sailfish,

and the Northern Lights like a coral reef
that never dies,

kept safely away from us.
"To the next life," he'd say, while pouring the whiskey.

"To hauling in Heaven's own salmon
and eating well."

Wednesday / 5:55 PST 8.5 ft. / 11:24 PST 5.9 ft.

By the sky's count, the land has seven seasons:
thaw, rain, green, heat, harvest, fall, and cold.

Of all of them, green is its favorite,
born from the clouds

and grown quickly
like our children grow so quickly.

But the ocean doesn't count that way.
It measures time by its sharks.

There are just three seasons, and they're all tied to hunger:
moving, arriving, being full.

Friday / 1:26 PST 3.9 ft. / 8:11 PST 8.9 ft.

A shark feels movement in the water—*Seal*—
and closes in below.

I find an old recording in a box,
buy a yard-sale record player.

It's a ballad, mournful,
barely there beneath the scratches:

two women singing harmony
about a ship going down in the sea.

The shark matches *Silhouette on surface* to *Attack*,
and the tone arm

skips
then drags through static . . .

Let's say the crew died peacefully
before the sharks arrived,

their souls swimming out of their bodies
and into this song.

Sunday / 3:11 PST 3.9 ft. / 9:37 PST 9.5 ft.

When his mom died, her photographs passed to my friend;
and when he died, they passed to me;

and when this town is gone,
replaced by another,

they'll remain—
dusted off for a retrospective;

and long before us, there were herons
gliding down to fish the river mouth,

the ocean admiring their stillness,
and spearing, and blue;

and long before herons,
there were coastal forests;

and before those trees, the moon,
pulling the tides from high to low, and back again.

Monday / 3:50 PST 3.9 ft. / 10:09 PST 9.8 ft.

I'm a gatherer of what's been gathered:
not the shore,

just one of the people on the edges;
not a house, just one of the drawers.

As purposes go,
it's not a bad purpose to have.

You can be the man choosing which wine for dinner,
or the woman cutting flowers for a vase.

I'll be the shelf the vase sits on.
I'll be the cupboard for the glasses and the plates ...

I have a black-and-white photo of a whitetip shark
taken near the inlet, so far from the open ocean

it must be lost,
or a curse,

or a warning.
I have an old song buried in a record I can't play.

I have high tide, and low tide,
and a thousand constellations ...

not stories or rituals
but maps to them.

So I begin.

Thank you to the editors of the following journals in which these poems, or earlier versions, sometimes under different titles, first appeared:

ellipsis . . . literature and art 50 (2014): "[The work of a shark is entirely body.]"; "[Spearing a seal means seven families eat]"; "[There must have been keepers of knowledge once]"; "[The man with jaws in his window is the most afraid]"; "[These long-ago scribes would have understood]"; "[Catch a shark in your net, you have to kill it,]"; "[There must have been a Council of Scribes once]" under the title "Reconstructing Fragments for *The Book of Sharks*."

Escape into Life (June 4, 2014): "["What do you do for a living?" is a complicated question]"; "[Some say sharks are the ocean's anger at us]"; "[Others focus on a different idea]"; "[In the oldest story we know of, sharks came first:]"; "[The best understanding I've heard was offered by a boy.]"; "[Given their name, it should be obvious]"; "[I'm a gatherer of what's been gathered:]" under the title "Gathering Pages for *The Book of Sharks*."

Rock & Sling 10 (2015): "[Before mountains rose from the ocean]"; "[Some say sharks are the ocean's blueprint for tools,]"; "[In the story once told to warn children, sharks were a curse]"; "[A blacktip, of course, has black-tipped fins,]"; "[The best explanation I know was offered by a boy.]"; "[Wear charms. Try remedies.]"; "[There is no body called *Carcharias* we look for in the sky.]" under the title "Seven Lessons from *The Book of Sharks*."

Rock & Sling 10 (2015): "[My friend told stories that weren't real stories at all]"; "[Another time, it was a clump of fur.]"; "[Or it might be three quick words,]"; "[Wear charms. Try remedies.]"; "[The cousin of a crow is a raven;]"; "[His house was always quiet]"; "[I'm not sure he knew it.]" under the title "A Chapter Missing from *The Book of Sharks*."

saltfront 3 (2015): "[The work of a shark is entirely body.]"; "[When stars are gathered in a pattern,]"; "[Most of us call the Big Dipper by its name.]"; "[By the sky's count, the land has seven seasons:]"; "[A shark feels movement in the water—*Seal*—]"; "[When his mom died, her photographs passed to my friend;]"; "[I'm a gatherer of what's been gathered:]" under the title "Tide Charts Listed in *The Book of Sharks*."

Terrain.org: A Journal of the Built & Natural Environments 34 (2013): "[Before mountains rose from the water]"; "[The oldest carving, though it's yet to be discovered,]"; "[Some say sharks are the ocean's anger at the sun]"; "[The best explanation I know was offered by a boy.]"; "[Divers know sharks share the water,]"; "[Given their name, it should be obvious:]"; "[There is no body called *Carcharias* we point to in the sky.]" under the title "Seven Pages from *The Book of Sharks*," winner of *Terrain.org*'s Annual Contest in Poetry, fall 2013.

"[The cousin of a shark is a manta ray;]"; "[In a story seldom remembered, sharks were ghosts]"; "[Under the first full moon of summer,]"; "[We have one such anchor on display in the museum,]"; "[and they're wrong about the skeletons,]"; "[Spearing a shark means seven days of work—]"; "[The edge of the sea is a teacher—] won the 2014 Robinson Jeffers/Tor House Foundation Poetry Prize and appeared in the Tor House Foundation Newsletter (Summer 2014) under the title "Seven Circles in *The Book of Sharks*."

"Gathering Pages for *The Book of Sharks*" appeared in *The Plume Anthology of Long-ish Poems 1*, edited by Andrew McFadyen-Ketchum and Matthew Silverman, Asheville, NC: Plume Editions/MadHat Press, 2018.

"Seven Circles in *The Book of Sharks*" appeared in the *Helicon West Anthology*, edited by Star Coulbrooke and Chadd VanZanten, Logan, UT: Helicon West Books, 2016.

"Seven Circles in *The Book of Sharks*" appeared in the anthology *Uncivilised Poetics*, edited by Em Strang, Nick Hunt, and Cate Chapman, London, UK: Dark Mountain Project, 2016.

"Seven Lessons from *The Book of Sharks*" received a 2015 Pushcart Prize nomination from *Rock & Sling*.

Rob Carney is originally from Washington state. He is the author of four previous collections, including *88 Maps* (Lost Horse Press 2015), which was named a finalist for the Washington State Book Award, and *Weather Report* (Somondoco Press 2006), which won the Utah Book Award for Poetry. His work has appeared in *Cave Wall*, *Columbia Journal*, *Sugar House Review*, *Terrain: A Journal of the Built & Natural Environments*, and dozens of others, as well as the Norton anthology *Flash Fiction Forward* (2006). In 2014 he received the Robinson Jeffers/Tor House Foundation Award for seven of the poems included here. He is a Professor of English and Literature at Utah Valley University and lives in Salt Lake City.